THE CIVIL RIGHTS MOVEMENT

by Max Winter

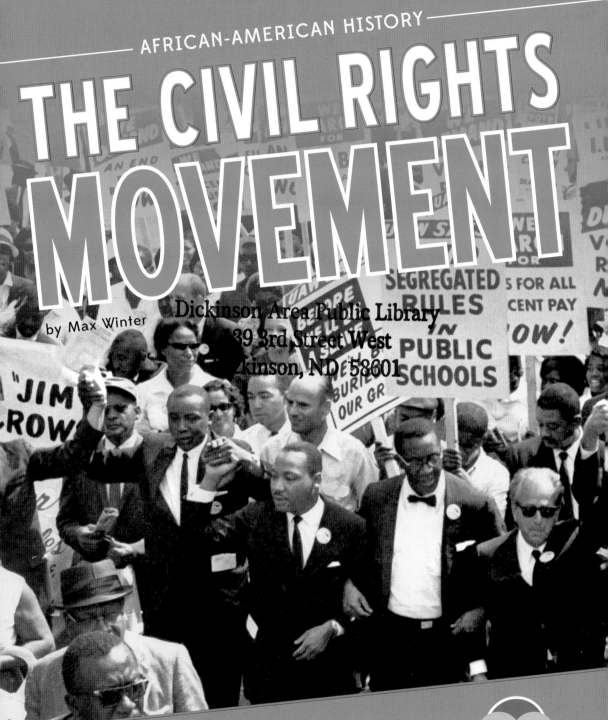

Content Consultant
Ibram X. Kendi, PhD
Assistant Professor, Africana Studies Department
University at Albany, SUNY

Core Library

An Imprint of Abdo Publishing
www.abdopublishing.com

Published by Abdo Publishing, a division of ABDO, PO Box 398166, Minneapolis, Minnesota 55439. Copyright © 2015 by Abdo Consulting Group, Inc. International copyrights reserved in all countries. No part of this book may be reproduced in any form without written permission from the publisher. Core Library™ is a trademark and logo of Abdo Publishing.

Printed in the United States of America,
North Mankato, Minnesota
022014
092014

Editor: Holly Saari
Series Designer: Becky Daum

Library of Congress Cataloging-in-Publication Data
Winter, Max.
 The Civil Rights Movement / by Max Winter.
   pages cm. -- (African-American History)
 ISBN 978-1-62403-145-8
1. African Americans--Civil rights--History--20th century--Juvenile literature. 2. Civil rights movements--United States--History--20th century--Juvenile literature. 3. United States--Race relations--Juvenile literature. I. Title.
 E185.61.W78 2014
 323.1196'073--dc23
                        2013027636

Photo Credits: AP Images, cover, 1, 9, 12, 15, 33, 34, 36; North Wind/North Wind Picture Archives, 4, 7; Library of Congress, 11; Thomas J. O'Halloran/Library of Congress, 18, 45; Bettmann/Corbis, 20, 24, 26, 40; Jim Bourdier/AP Images, 28; Red Line Editorial, 23, 38; Gene Herrick/AP Images, 30

CONTENTS

CHAPTER ONE

A HISTORY OF SLAVERY AND DISCRIMINATION

In 1619 the first African slaves arrived in the British colonies. They were brought against their will and forced to work the land for no pay. This marked the beginning of hundreds of years of unjust treatment of African Americans in what would become the United States.

Slaves lived in terrible conditions. They were often poorly fed. They worked long hours in the hot sun.

Slavery lasted in the United States for more than 200 years.

Slavery was practiced all over the growing nation. But the majority of slaves worked in the South on farms or large plantations. Slaves were considered the property of their masters. Slaves could be whipped if they disobeyed their masters. Slavery spread throughout the 1600s, 1700s, and 1800s.

Slavery Ends

In 1865 the Thirteenth Amendment was added to the Constitution. An amendment adds to or changes a governing document. The Thirteenth Amendment abolished slavery in the United States. African Americans were now free. But they were not treated as equals to whites. Some freed slaves said their lives were even worse after they were freed. Former slaves did not have homes. They also did not have jobs or an income. They could not afford to buy their own land to work. Finding food and shelter was difficult for many. When African Americans did find jobs, they often got the most difficult work for the lowest pay.

After slavery ended, African Americans often still worked in the fields of white farmers.

However, this period did bring African Americans more civil rights under the law. In 1868 the Fourteenth Amendment was added to the Constitution. It made African Americans US citizens. It granted all citizens equal protection under the law. In 1870 the Fifteenth Amendment was added. It gave African-American men the right to vote.

These amendments were supposed to help African Americans gain freedom and be treated equally. But African Americans still faced discrimination, especially in the South. African Americans sometimes worked the land of their former slave owners. But the former masters did not give the workers much in return. Discrimination and racism continued. African Americans earned little money and lived in poverty.

Jim Crow Laws

In the late 1870s, cities and states began to pass laws that were meant to keep African Americans separate from whites. These laws were called Jim

---

Voting Trouble

African Americans faced challenges when trying to vote. They were often forced to pass literacy tests. Most of the judges were prejudiced against African Americans. The judges often gave African-American citizens unfair tests and failing grades. That meant they could not vote.

Jim Crow laws kept whites apart from African Americans in transportation waiting rooms.

Crow laws. Most Jim Crow laws were passed in the South. The Jim Crow laws affected most areas of African Americans' lives. African Americans could not eat in the same restaurants as whites. They could not sleep in the same hotels. They could not use the same bathrooms.

In 1896 a court case called *Plessy v. Ferguson* came before the US Supreme Court. This case was meant to challenge segregation in Louisiana train cars. The Supreme Court ruled that segregation was allowed in public places as long as each race had equal facilities. The ruling became known as "separate but equal." But the reality was that separate facilities for African Americans were usually far from equal.

The NAACP

In 1909 African-American W. E. B. Du Bois and others founded the National Association for the Advancement of Colored People (NAACP). Its goals were to make sure all people had equality and civil rights. It also fought to end racial discrimination and hatred. The NAACP focused much of their efforts on ending Jim Crow laws. The group filed lawsuits against segregation. It also worked to stop the

Du Bois hoped the NAACP would be able to end segregation.

lynchings of African Americans. A lynching was when a mob of white people murdered an African American, usually by hanging.

CHAPTER TWO

BROWN V. BOARD OF EDUCATION

Jim Crow laws meant African-American children could not attend the same schools as white children. Schools for African Americans were far from equal to those of whites. African-American schools received much less money. They had fewer supplies such as books. Because of this, African-American students received worse educations than white students.

African-American students had to attend separate schools from whites.

Early Desegregation Work

In the 1930s, the NAACP started working to end school segregation. The leader in this battle was African-American lawyer Charles Hamilton Houston. Houston won important cases. At the time, African Americans who wished to attend law school in Missouri were not allowed to do so. They had to attend law school out of state. Houston's work changed this. This victory and others helped lay the groundwork for later, larger court decisions.

The Beginnings of the *Brown* Case

In 1950 Oliver Brown and several other African-American parents tried to enroll their children in white schools in Topeka, Kansas. Topeka had 18 elementary schools for white children. It had only four for African Americans. The schools were hard to reach for students who lived far away. Brown and the other parents were not allowed to enroll their children in the white schools.

Oliver Brown's daughter Linda was denied admission to an all-white school.

Brown and the parents filed a lawsuit against the Topeka Board of Education. They wanted to stop school segregation. In the case, the NAACP argued that segregation went against the Fourteenth Amendment. The federal district court ruled against the parents in 1951. The court stated the white and African-American schools were equal in the quality of education they gave. The fact that African-American

15

The Little Rock Nine

In 1957 nine African-American students tried to enter Little Rock Central High School in Little Rock, Arkansas. Those against integration protested violently against this and captured national attention. President Dwight Eisenhower stepped in. He was worried the students might get hurt. He called in the US Army to protect the students. In order to remain safe, the students had to be escorted to and from class.

schools had poor resources did not matter. Therefore, schools could stay segregated without damaging the students. Brown and the other plaintiffs appealed to the Supreme Court in 1952.

Five Cases Combined

Around the same time, African-American students in Virginia, South Carolina, and Delaware were denied requests to attend all-white schools. Four lawsuits were filed. The courts ruled against the plaintiffs. The decisions were appealed to the Supreme Court in 1952. These cases were very similar to the case from Topeka, Kansas.

The five cases were combined in *Brown v. Board of Education.* The Supreme Court heard them as one case.

Arguing the Case

Several lawyers argued for the plaintiffs in front of the Supreme Court justices. Thurgood Marshall was one of them. He worked with the NAACP's Legal Defense and Educational Fund. The lawyers said the Fourteenth Amendment made discrimination in public places, such as schools, illegal. They also argued that segregation of schools had a negative effect on African-American students, who

Thurgood Marshall

Thurgood Marshall had a great career before his work on *Brown v. Board of Education.* In 1933 he graduated first in his class from Howard University Law School. In 1940 he founded the NAACP's Legal Defense and Educational Fund. Marshall won several victories in cases that helped stop discrimination. In 1967 Marshall became the first African American on the Supreme Court.

After Brown v. Board of Education, schools were slowly integrated.

were treated as if they were inferior to whites and given inferior resources.

Those in favor of segregation argued the Constitution did not state white and African-American children had to attend the same schools. They said segregation did not hurt African-American children. They also argued the states should be allowed to make their own rules about segregation.

Overturning School Segregation

In 1954 all nine Supreme Court justices voted in favor of the plaintiffs in the case. The Court had overturned school segregation. Schools were now forced to integrate. However, conditions did not change overnight for African-American students. Integration did not officially begin until the following year. Still, many people mark the beginning of the civil rights movement as 1954. The ruling against school segregation gave people hope that things could change. They were eager to continue fighting for it.

CHAPTER THREE

BOYCOTTING, SITTING, AND RIDING FOR CHANGE

The purpose of the civil rights movement was for African Americans to gain equality in the United States. The movement included acts of civil disobedience to protest discrimination and segregation. Civil disobedience involves refusing to obey unjust laws or rules. Acts of civil disobedience are often peaceful. But they attract attention because they disrupt everyday life.

Bus segregation forced African Americans to sit in the backs of city buses.

Montgomery Bus Boycott

On December 1, 1955, Rosa Parks got on a city bus in Montgomery, Alabama. She sat down in a seat in the first row of the African-American section. At the time, African Americans were expected to sit at the backs of city buses. Soon the bus filled up. The bus driver then asked Parks to give her seat to a white person. Parks refused. She was eventually arrested.

Parks's act of civil disobedience inspired others. Soon after, African Americans boycotted the buses in Montgomery. They organized other means of transportation. Some used carpools. Others walked. Some people walked miles a

Rosa Parks

Rosa Parks was born in 1913. Around age 20, she began working for African-American civil rights. She joined the NAACP. After her protest in 1955, she became famous nationally. But she lost her job at a department store because of her actions. In 1987 she cofounded the Rosa and Raymond Parks Institute for Self-Development. It continues to educate young people about the civil rights movement.

Locations of Key Civil Rights Events

This map shows events that occurred within the civil rights movement and after, from 1955 to 1979. The civil rights movement included many acts of peaceful civil disobedience, such as Rosa Parks's. However, sometimes protests erupted into violence. White violence against African Americans and civil rights activists, such as lynchings and beatings, also occurred. Connect what you read in this chapter to the dots on the map. How does this map help you better understand the civil rights movement?

day to avoid buses. The boycott helped the civil rights movement gain national attention.

In November 1956, the US Supreme Court ruled that bus segregation was unconstitutional. The Court stated segregation violated the Fourteenth

African Americans participated in sit-ins to protest segregation at lunch counters and restaurants.

Amendment. It guaranteed equal treatment under the law. Buses in Montgomery then had to be integrated.

Sit-Ins

In 1960 another act of civil disobedience occurred. One afternoon four African-American college students sat down at a lunch counter in Greensboro, North Carolina. The restaurant was for whites only. The students knew this. After not serving the students, the owner asked them to leave. But they wouldn't. They were taking part in a sit-in to protest the restaurant's segregation.

The owner called the police. When the police arrived, they tried to force the students to leave. The students still would not move. The police eventually gave up because the students weren't doing anything harmful. The event brought even more attention to the civil rights movement. Soon other people were staging similar sit-ins in more than 50 cities across the country.

Freedom Rides

In 1946 the Supreme Court ruled it was unconstitutional to segregate public

The Lynching of Emmett Till

In 1955 14-year-old Emmett Till visited a family member in the small town of Money, Mississippi. While he was visiting, someone said he whistled at a young white woman in a grocery store. Soon after, he was kidnapped, beaten, and shot in the head. The murderers were found not guilty by an all-white jury. The murder of the young boy and the lack of punishment for his killers united civil rights activists in anger.

One of the buses was set on fire during the Freedom Rides.

transportation that traveled between states. In 1961 approximately 400 people of different races began the Freedom Rides to test this ruling. They rode buses from Virginia to Mississippi.

They found out the ruling was not being obeyed. African Americans on the buses were beaten. Despite their injuries, these riders got a lot of press during the five months they rode buses. As a result of their actions, the Interstate Commerce Commission issued new rules banning segregation in buses traveling between states.

In 1960 a *New York Times* article discussed the sit-in in Greensboro, North Carolina. The first part of the article pointed out the civil rights movement in the South was growing:

> *Negro student demonstrations against segregated eating facilities have raised grave questions in the South over the future of the region's race relations. A sounding of opinion in the affected areas showed that much more might be involved than the matter of the Negro's right to sit at a lunch counter for a coffee break.*
>
> *The demonstrations were generally dismissed at first as another college fad. . . . This opinion lost adherents, however, as the movement spread. . . .*
>
> *Some whites wrote off the episodes as the work of "outside agitators." But even they conceded that the seeds of dissent had fallen in fertile soil.*
>
> Source: Claude Sitton. "Negro Sitdowns Stir Fear of Wider Unrest in the South." The New York Times on the Web. *The New York Times Company, n.d. Web. Accessed July 15, 2013.*

Changing Minds

Many people across the country read the *New York Times*. They have different opinions and beliefs. How do you think this text would be different if it was written only for those involved in the civil rights movement? Write the new article and compare how the two are different.

CHAPTER FOUR

THE IMPACT OF MARTIN LUTHER KING JR.

No leader had a greater impact on the civil rights movement than Martin Luther King Jr. King was born in 1929 in Atlanta, Georgia. He became a Christian minister in 1954. King believed people should love their enemies. He believed in using nonviolence to protest injustice.

For many, King was the face of the civil rights movement.

King helped unite people with shared interests to work toward a common cause.

Role in Bus Boycott

King's first major role in the civil rights movement was in helping organize the defense of Rosa Parks in 1955. He led the Montgomery Improvement Association. This was the group that helped organize and run the Montgomery bus boycott. King was a great speaker. His words inspired those in the boycott to continue. During the boycott, King's home was bombed. But he continued his role in the boycott until the Supreme Court ruled bus segregation was unconstitutional.

The SCLC

In 1957 King and others formed the Southern Christian Leadership Conference (SCLC). The group organized the protests that were taking place in cities across the South. The SCLC was involved in a number of actions that drew attention to the civil rights movement. The SCLC staged sit-ins at several places. It also organized boycotts of stores that practiced segregation.

Birmingham Desegregates

King helped organize boycotts, sit-ins, and marches in Birmingham, Alabama, in the early 1960s. The protesters were arrested at first. Court cases and negotiations between city leaders, King, and the SCLC followed. Finally the city segregation policies were reversed. The whole city desegregated. This accomplishment is considered one of King's greatest.

March on Washington

On August 28, 1963, the March on Washington for Jobs and Freedom was held in Washington, DC. It was a call for civil and economic rights for African Americans. The March on Washington was one of the largest public demonstrations in US history. More than 200,000 people of many races gathered at the Washington Monument. They then marched to the Lincoln Memorial.

Once there, speakers and musicians spoke and sang for equal rights. King gave his inspiring and unforgettable

Protests and Arrests

King was arrested several times throughout the civil rights movement. In October 1960, King was arrested and put in prison briefly. He and 33 other African Americans held a sit-in at a department store restaurant. In 1963 King and others held a demonstration in Birmingham, Alabama. Police broke up the event. The officers turned dogs loose on the protesters. The police also fired water hoses at the crowd. King was again arrested. Yet it did not stop him from continuing his work.

King was arrested several times due to his activities in the civil rights movement.

"I Have a Dream" speech. He spoke of his goals of equality and freedom for African Americans.

Leader of the Movement

After the march, King was recognized across the country as a key leader of the civil rights movement. He spoke up for civil rights at many events. He continued to take part in protests. Other African-American groups began to criticize him because he

King spoke before a sea of people at the March on Washington.

focused too much on nonviolence. They argued his peaceful methods were not aggressive enough for the problems they hoped to solve. But nonviolence remained a central part of King's message and the movement.

King's "I Have a Dream" speech is one of the most famous speeches in US history. It marked a key moment for the civil rights movement. Those who heard it felt a connection with the dreams King stated:

> I have a dream that one day this nation will rise up and live out the true meaning of its creed: "We hold these truths to be self-evident: that all men are created equal."
>
> I have a dream that one day on the red hills of Georgia the sons of former slaves and the sons of former slave owners will be able to sit down together at a table of brotherhood. . . .
>
> I have a dream that my four children will one day live in a nation where they will not be judged by the color of their skin but by the content of their character.

Source: Martin Luther King Jr. "Martin Luther King's Speech: I Have a Dream—The Full Text." ABC News. ABC News Network, n.d. Web. Accessed June 26, 2013.

What's the Big Idea?

Take a close look at this speech. What is the main idea King is trying to communicate? Pick out two details that support this main point. How do King's words fit in with the civil rights movement's goals?

CHAPTER FIVE

THE LEGACY OF THE MOVEMENT

During the civil rights movement, countless people fought for equality. They worked to improve the living conditions of African Americans. The movement's actions were not always successful. Activists faced violence and setbacks. Yet meaningful laws resulted from the movement. And the lives of many African Americans were changed for the better.

Marches, protests, and demonstrations helped bring about civil rights laws.

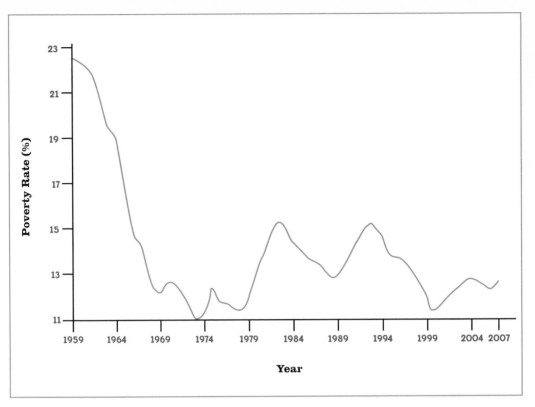

Poverty Decreases
The graph above shows how the percentage of African-American families living in poverty has changed since 1959. How do you think the civil rights movement contributed to this change? What information from Chapter Five helps support this?

The Civil Rights Act

The Civil Rights Act was passed in 1964. It made it illegal for any employer or public facility to discriminate on the basis of race. The act did not pass through Congress without debate. But it did help bring the problem of discrimination to the minds of politicians. African Americans could now eat in the same restaurants as whites. They could not be denied a job because of the color of their skin.

The Voting Rights Act

In 1965 the Voting Rights Act became law. The Fifteenth Amendment gave African-American men the right to vote. But African Americans still faced challenges at the polls. This act made it illegal to discriminate against African Americans who voted. They no longer had to pass literacy tests in order to vote.

The EEOC

The Civil Rights Act of 1964 created the Equal Employment Opportunity Commission (EEOC). Its main goal was to guarantee all citizens equal rights in the workplace. It wanted to make sure African Americans would not be discriminated against during job interviews. It worked to make sure African Americans were not treated poorly at work because of their skin color. The EEOC continues to strive toward these goals today.

President Lyndon Johnson signs the Voting Rights Act into law.

Movement Comes to an End

The civil rights movement is often thought of as ending in 1965 after the Voting Rights Act was passed. Still, many people kept working for civil rights. King was one of them. But on April 4, 1968, James Earl Ray shot King as he stood on the balcony of a local motel. Ray was racist and against integration. Riots broke out after King was assassinated. The Civil Rights Act of 1968 passed through Congress just days after King was killed. Still, King's early death was a huge loss to the fight for civil rights.

The challenges African Americans faced did not end with the civil rights movement. Today, many people continue to work for equal treatment.

IMPORTANT DATES

1619

Slavery begins in the British colonies of the present-day United States.

1865

The Thirteenth Amendment to the US Constitution abolishes slavery.

1954

The Supreme Court rules in *Brown v. Board of Education* that school segregation is unconstitutional.

1961

Freedom Riders test if segregation still exists in public transportation by traveling on buses between states.

1963

At the March on Washington, Martin Luther King Jr. gives his "I Have a Dream" speech.

1964

The Civil Rights Act is passed. It makes racial discrimination in private businesses or public spaces illegal.

1955

Rosa Parks is arrested for refusing to give her bus seat to a white person.

1956

The Montgomery bus boycott ends when the Supreme Court rules bus segregation is unconstitutional.

1960

Four college students hold the first sit-in at a lunch counter in Greensboro, North Carolina.

1965

The Voting Rights Act is passed. It prevents racial discrimination at the polls.

1965

The official civil rights movement comes to an end.

1968

King is assassinated in Memphis, Tennessee.

STOP AND THINK

Why Do I Care?

Most of the events described in this book happened more than 40 years ago. But that doesn't mean they don't affect your life. People continue to discuss the civil rights movement and its meaning for today. How might your life be different if the civil rights movement had never happened?

You Are There

Imagine you were present to hear Martin Luther King Jr.'s "I Have a Dream" speech in 1963. What would you notice? How would you feel about being there? Write a letter to a friend that describes your experience.

Tell the Tale

Chapter Three describes several key events that occurred during the civil rights movement. Retell one of these events in 200 words. Be sure to establish the setting, give the sequence of events, and offer a conclusion.

Surprise Me

This book discusses the civil rights movement, which occurred during the 1950s and 1960s. After reading this book, what two or three facts about this period did you find most surprising? Why were they surprising to you? Write two or three sentences about each fact.

GLOSSARY

appeal
to have a higher court review a lower court's decision

boycott
the refusal to buy goods or take part in an activity in order to protest injustice

civil rights
the rights and freedoms of each citizen of the United States

discriminate
to treat someone unfairly based on differences such as race or gender

integrate
to bring people who were once segregated back into another group

plaintiff
a person or party who begins a legal action or lawsuit

segregate
to involuntarily separate or keep people apart from another group

sit-in
the act of occupying seats in a segregated place to protest discrimination

unconstitutional
not in agreement with the constitution of a government

LEARN MORE

Books

Dunn, Joeming. *Martin Luther King Jr.* Edina, MN: Magic Wagon, 2009.

McWhorter, Diane. *A Dream of Freedom: The Civil Rights Movement from 1954 to 1968*. New York: Scholastic, 2004.

Morrison, Toni. *Remember: The Journey to School Integration*. Boston: Houghton Mifflin, 2004.

Websites

To learn more about African-American History, visit **booklinks.abdopublishing.com**. These links are routinely monitored and updated to provide the most current information available. Visit **www.mycorelibrary.com** for free additional tools for teachers and students.

INDEX

ABOUT THE AUTHOR

Max Winter has written and edited many books about social studies and science for young readers. The subjects of these books have ranged from the Statue of Liberty to building one's own radio.